Creature Comparisons

Bears

Tracey Crawford

www.heinemann.co.uk/library
Visit our website to find out more information about **Heinemann Library** books.

To order:
☎ Phone 44 (0) 1865 888066
🖹 Send a fax to 44 (0) 1865 314091
💻 Visit the Heinemann Bookshop at www.heinemann.co.uk/library to browse our catalogue and order online.

First published in Great Britain by Heinemann Library, Halley Court, Jordan Hill, Oxford OX2 8EJ, part of Harcourt Education. Heinemann is a registered trademark of Harcourt Education Ltd.

© Harcourt Education Ltd 2007.
The moral right of the proprietor has been asserted.

Editorial: Tracey Crawford, Cassie Mayer, Dan Nunn, and Sarah Chappelow
Design: Jo Hinton-Malivoire
Picture Research: Tracy Cummins and Tracey Engel
Production: Duncan Gilbert

Originated by Chroma Graphics (Overseas) Pte. Ltd
Printed and bound in China by South China Printing Company

10 digit ISBN 0 431 18226 4
13 digit ISBN 978 0 431 18226 1

11 10 09 08 07
10 9 8 7 6 5 4 3 2 1

British Library Cataloguing in Publication Data
Crawford, Tracey
    Bears. - (Creature comparisons)
    1.Bears - Juvenile literature
    I.Title
    599.7'8
A full catalogue record for this book is available from the British Library.

Acknowledgements
The publishers would like to thank the following for permission to reproduce photographs: Alamy pp. **9** (John Schwieder), **10** (Garry DeLong), **13** (Balan), **17** (Winston Fraser); Corbis pp. **4** (bird, Arthur Morris), **5** (A. & S. Carey/zefa), **7** (Gunter Marx Photography), **14** (Ralph A. Clevenger), **15** (Keren Su), **18** (Michael DeYoung), **22** (polar bear, David E. Myers/zefa); Howie Garber p. **19**; Getty Images pp. **4** (fish), **6** (PhotoDisc), **11** (Roy Toft), **16** (Andy Rouse), **20** (Eastcott Momatiuk), **21** (Hans Strand); Naturepl.com p. **12**; Science Photo Library p. **22** (Sun bear, Art Wolfe); Carlton Ward p. **4** (snake, frog).

Cover photograph of a giant panda reproduced with permission of Corbis/Tim Davis and a brown bear reproduced with permission of Corbis/Royalty Free. Back cover photograph of a polar bear reproduced with permission of Corbis/Michael DeYoung.

Every effort has been made to contact copyright holders of any material reproduced in this book. Any omissions will be rectified in subsequent printings if notice is given to the publishers.

Contents

There are many types of animals.

Bears are one type of animal.
Bears are mammals.

All bears have fur.

All bears have paws and claws.

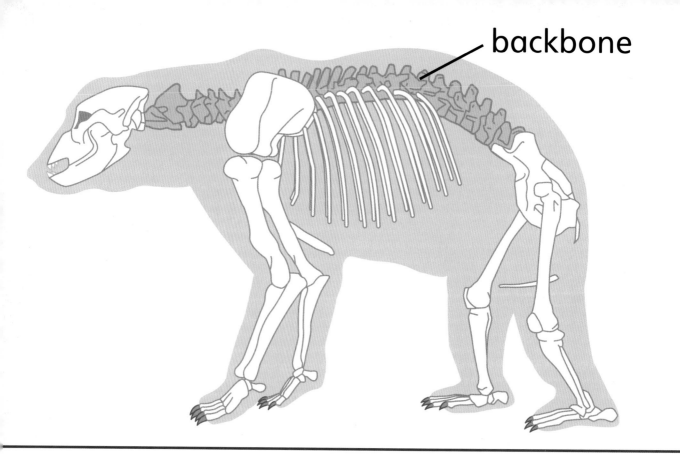

backbone

All bears have a backbone.

All baby bears get milk from
their mother.

All bears walk on four legs.

All bears can stand on two feet.

Most bears sleep during the winter.

But this bear does not.

Some bears eat fish.

But these bears do not.

Some bears are big.

Some bears are small.

Some bears swim.

Some bears climb.

Every bear is different.

Every bear is special.

Bear facts

Polar bears have two layers of fur. This helps keep them warm.

Sun bears spend most of their time in trees. They have long claws. This helps them climb.

Picture glossary

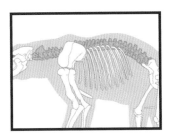

backbone the part of the skeleton that goes from the head to the tail

Index

Notes to parents and teachers
Before reading
Talk to the children about bears. Has anyone seen a bear on television or in a zoo? Have they got a favourite teddy bear?

After reading
Share the tale "We're going on a bear hunt", joining in with actions, e.g. Swish swash through the water; Squelch, squelch through the mud, etc. Play the Bear Circle game. Tell the children to sit in a circle facing inwards. Give each child a name of a bear, either brown bear, grizzly bear, or polar bear. Call out one of the bears and those children stand up and move outside the circle. On command they move around the circle in a given direction e.g. crawl, lumber, and run. On the command "Into the cave", they race back to their places and sit down.
Draw a large outline of a bear on a large sheet of brown paper and cut it out. Cover the bear with scrunched square of brown tissue paper. Use black scrunched tissue paper for the eyes and mouth and a large bead painted black for the nose.

Titles in the *Creature Comparisons* series include:

Hardback   0 431 18226 4

Hardback   0 431 18225 6

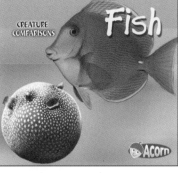

Hardback   0 431 18224 8

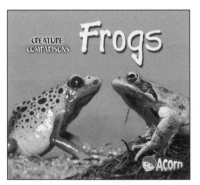

Hardback   0 431 18228 0

Hardback   0 431 18223 X

Hardback   0 431 18227 2

Find out about other titles from Heinemann Library on our website www.heinemann.co.uk/library